Team Reader

The Trea
of T

Dear Diego,

Happy reading!

With best wishes,

Jemma Watt

Oct 2022

Illustrated by Andrew Smith

Ernst Klett Sprachen
Stuttgart

Augmented

You can access the audiobook on your mobile phone or a tablet. Download and install the Klett Augmented app.

Scan the title page (p 1) using the camera on your mobile phone/tablet. Then download the audio files for each chapter.

Install the Klett Augmented app on your device

Start picture recognition and scan the title page

Download files and use them straight away or save them for later

Bookmark

The bookmark can help you with difficult words. These words are marked with * in the text.
In case you lose the bookmark, you can download it again at *www.klett-sprachen.de* by entering the following code in the search field: **664nm57**

Contents

Team Read
Choose one of the following characters and tick the box. Read only your character's chapters and those chapters that *everybody* has to read.

Of course ...
You *can* always read the whole story and discover everything that's going on for yourself!

Read chapters for (A):
1, 2, 3, 6, 9, 10, 11,
14, 15

ALICIA & SAMMY
Choose to follow Alicia & Sammy if you do not read books very often or if you feel that long texts in English are confusing. Alicia & Sammy help to find the keys to the treasure. But suddenly they are followed by a strange man. Can they escape and trick the man? Will they be able to find a key ...? ☐

Read chapters for Ⓔ:
1, 2, 4, 7, 9, 10, 12,
14, 15

ELLA

Ella is looking for a key to the treasure inside the old house – but what she finds ... If you sometimes read books *or* if English is not really difficult for you, follow Ella's chapters. Can she find a key and is she really alone or is there somebody else in the house? ☐

Read chapters for Ⓡ:
1, 2, 5, 8, 9, 10, 13,
14, 15

ROHAN

Rohan is looking for the treasure keys in the gardens – and finds a gigantic stone teapot. If you read a lot *or* if English is really easy for you, read Rohan's chapters and discover if he can really solve all the riddles and find out where the treasure lies. ☐

Chapter 1

Something soft hit Ella on the back of her head.

"*Alicia!*" Ella picked* up the old teddy bear from the attic floor and frowned* at her younger sister. "Stop throwing things at me, or I'll ..."

The doorbell rang from downstairs.

"You'd better get it," said Alicia. "Mum and Dad are outside."

Ella went downstairs to answer the door to a twelve-year-old boy in a football T-shirt and shorts.

"Hi!" said Rohan, Ella's best friend. "Do you want to go to the park?"

Ella sighed*. "I can't. Dad's making me tidy the attic with Alicia."

"Oh. Well, I'll help you, then we can go out after!" Rohan smiled.

They both went up to the attic.

"Where's your sister?" asked Rohan.

Ella looked out of the window and saw Alicia walking away from the house with her small brown and white dog. "Urgh! She's outside with Sammy! I can't believe it. She knows if I tell Mum and Dad, then we'll both get into trouble."

Rohan’s shoe hit something in the floor. “Ow!” he cried in surprise. He picked up a nail* and a piece* of the wooden* floor came up with it. Rohan looked down. “Ella!” Rohan was excited. “Look at this.”

"What is it?"

"There's something hidden* in the floor!" Carefully, he picked up an old teapot*. Rohan opened the lid* and looked inside. Pulling out a yellow piece of paper, he read the words:

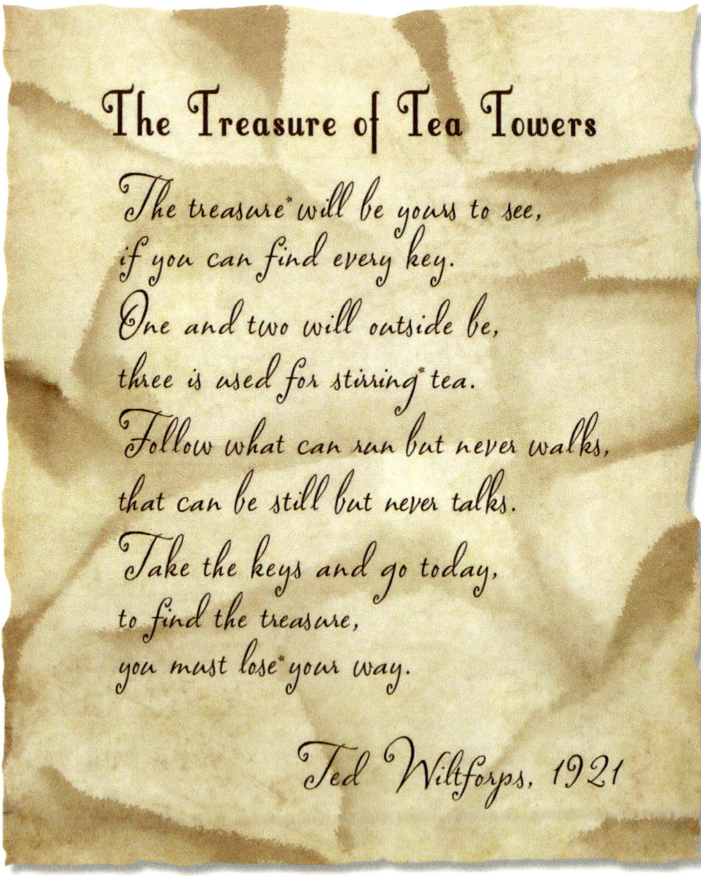

The Treasure of Tea Towers

The treasure* will be yours to see,
if you can find every key.
One and two will outside be,
three is used for stirring* tea.
Follow what can run but never walks,
that can be still but never talks.
Take the keys and go today,
to find the treasure,
you must lose* your way.

Ted Wiltforps, 1921

Rohan looked at Ella with wide eyes. *"Treasure*!"*

"Tea Towers!" said Ella. "That's the old house up on the hill."

"Have you ever heard of a treasure there?"

"No... let's ask Mum or Dad about it later. But don't tell Alicia, it can be our secret*!"

An hour later Alicia came back to the attic, just before her dad came upstairs.

"Well, this all looks a lot tidier," he said, looking around.

"Thanks Dad, we worked really hard!" said Alicia. Ella's face turned* red and she was about to say something when Rohan quickly spoke.

"Mr Wilson," he said, "do you know that big old house up on the hill?"

"Tea Towers? Yes, an interesting old place. Empty* now. Old Mr Potts who used to live there is at the care* home in the village."

"Why are you interested in it?" asked Alicia, crossing her arms.

"No reason," said Ella, smiling at Rohan. "Can we go out now, Dad?"

"Yes, after lunch."

"Let's go to Tea Towers!" whispered Ella as soon as her sister had left the attic.

Rohan frowned. "We wouldn't know where to look for the keys... *two are outside*... that's got to be a big space*. And what *can run but never walks*? A train?"

Ella looked at the floor. "There are no train lines* up on the hill... Let's go and see Mr Potts, maybe he knows something about it all!"

Chapter 2

"Mr Potts doesn't often have visitors," said the carer* to Ella and Rohan. "I'm sure he'll be happy!" She took them into a room where old people sat in groups watching TV or playing cards and board games. "There he is over there." She pointed* to a bald* man in glasses wearing a shirt, asleep in a wheelchair* far away from the others.

The pair walked up to the old man. Out of the window they saw Tea Towers, sitting on top of a hill with its grey stone* walls.

"Hello," said Ella.

Mr Potts woke up and looked at the children in surprise. "Hello... are you looking for somebody?"

"Err, ...I'm Ella, ... and this is my friend Rohan. We want to talk to you about Tea Towers."

"And ask you about the hidden treasure," added Rohan.

"Hidden treasure?" Mr Potts laughed. "You two have been watching too much TV."

"Well, how do you explain this?" Ella handed* him the piece of paper from the attic.

Mr Potts slowly read the words on the page. "Ted Wiltforps? Don't know him. Keys... keys... I remember my grandfather saying something about keys. He used to own a chain* of tea shops all across the country, called *'Potts' Tea Shops'*. You may have heard of them?"

"Er, sorry, no," said Ella. "What did he say about the keys?"

Mr Potts gave the letter back to her. "I can't remember."

"Well... can we go to Tea Towers and look for the treasure?" asked Rohan.

"Hmm...it's empty... Alright, go to the house if you want.

I don't think you'll find anything there. Just don't get yourselves hurt or in trouble."

"Fantastic!" Rohan jumped up and down with excitement*.

"Great!" Ella smiled. "Oh, umm, one more thing. What can run but cannot walk... do you know what that's all about?"

Mr Potts sneezed*. *"Aaah chooo!"*

"A nose!" cried Rohan. "A nose can run!"

Ella rolled her eyes. "We can't go looking for a nose!"

Mr Potts began coughing. "What are you... --*cough, cough* -- ... bring me some water from over there, will you."

Rohan poured* some water from a bottle into a glass and stared* at it. "This is it..." he suddenly cried. "... it can run in a river... and it can be still, like in this glass... but it can't walk!"

"WATER!"

"Yes!" Ella's eyes lit* up. "You are right. It must be water."
Ella and Rohan couldn't wait to get to Tea Towers to start looking for the treasure. After saying goodbye to Mr Potts, they went to leave and walked straight* into a man and woman in their thirties, wearing suits*.

"Watch* where you're going!" said the woman, frowning.

"What's this..." said the man, picking up the piece of paper with the riddle* that Ella had dropped on the floor.

"That's mine, thanks," said Ella, grabbing* the paper back as the man looked at the words on the page.

"Come on," said the woman, taking the man by the arm.

"They don't look very friendly," whispered Rohan as he looked over his shoulder. "Hey! They're going to talk to Mr Potts!"

"That's strange," said Ella. "The carer said he doesn't get many visitors. Let's get out of here!"

Twenty minutes later, Rohan and Ella arrived at a pair of open, large, old metal gates*.

"Hey, isn't that Alicia's?" Rohan pointed to a bike parked against a tree. Sammy ran out to them from inside the gates, followed by Alicia.

"What are you doing here?" said Ella, crossing her arms.

"I knew you two were up* to something, asking Dad about Tea Towers, so I thought I'd check it out! It looks really old. So, what's going on?"

Ella shook* her head. "We're not telling you."

"Oh come on!" said Alicia. "If you don't tell me, I'll tell Mum and Dad you broke* into someone's house."

"She could help us find the keys," said Rohan, turning* to Ella. "If we split* up, we can find them quicker."

"Keys to what?" asked Alicia.

"Fine!" Ella took the riddle and showed it to her sister. "We found this in the attic and went to see Mr Potts, there are three keys to a treasure."

"What can run but never walks..." read Alicia.

"It's water!" said Rohan. "We have to look for water, two keys outside and one inside. Then we have to use them to find the treasure."

"Why does it say we have to 'lose* our way'?" asked Alicia.

"We don't know..." said Ella. "Let's find the keys first. I'll try and get inside the house while you two look for water outside."

"Let's hide* our bikes behind the trees," said Rohan. "Just in case* anyone comes and tells us we can't be here. We'll look for the keys and meet back here at the gates!"

Chapter 3

After hiding her bike, Alicia turned left inside the gates with Sammy and walked through a small wood*. Sammy found some sticks* that he brought to Alicia.

"I can't play now Sammy, I'm busy!" she told him. "We need to look for water!"

There was no water anywhere and the woods felt cold out of the sun.

Soon, they came to a large area of grass. Alicia saw the sun shining* down on a small pond* in front of her.

"A pond!" she said, smiling at Sammy. "Let's look for the keys!"

They ran over and Alicia began looking all around the edge* of the water.

"There's just grass," she thought to herself as she ran her hands through her dark hair.

Suddenly she heard a voice. A man's voice. Thinking quickly, her eyes looked for a place to hide. She jumped behind a bush, pulling Sammy behind.

"Sssshhh!" she whispered to Sammy, holding him close*.

Looking up from the bush, she saw a man walking around and talking on his mobile phone.

"Who is that?" she whispered to herself. She held her breath*, hoping that the man would not walk around to her side of the pond.

Thankfully he turned and walked away. She waited for a few minutes and then went back to the pond. The man was gone.

The keys – she still needed to find the keys. Carefully, she started looking around the pond again.

Suddenly, she heard a sound behind her...

Alicia screamed in shock as somebody grabbed* her arm.

Chapter 4

Ella walked up to a large wooden front door. The door wasn't locked*. Looking behind her, she went inside.

The house was dusty* and in a bad condition*. Ella felt uncomfortable. "Right," she thought to herself, "I need to find water! Maybe the key is by a sink*."

She walked past the stairs into a room at the back of the house. An old sofa was in the middle of the room along with large windows looking out onto the garden.

"No water here," thought Ella. "This looks like it was a living room."

She made her way through several* other rooms until she came to a bathroom. The room looked like something from the 1970s and there was no sign of any hundred-year-old secrets. Ella turned around, walked back through the other rooms and went upstairs.

The stairs led* to several bedrooms and a few more bathrooms.

"It doesn't look like there's anything here," thought Ella.

She was about to go downstairs when she heard the front door open. With a gasp*, she quickly turned and hid in the nearest bedroom, not wanting to be caught by whoever this was.

Ella heard footsteps. "I think they've gone into the living room," she thought, her hands shaking*. She hurried back down the stairs. Before she could get to the front door, the footsteps were coming closer*. Panicking, Ella opened a door to her right and ran down another staircase. She found herself in a large kitchen.

This room was also dirty and dusty – just like the other rooms. A mouse ran across the floor and Ella covered* her mouth with her hands to stop herself screaming. The staircase door above her opened with a small sound.

Ella needed somewhere to hide, but the room was almost empty. She noticed* a large cupboard and raced towards it.

The cupboard was full of spiders' webs* that covered Ella's face. Closing her eyes in fear*, she pulled the door closed and moved backwards.

The back of the cupboard moved and suddenly... there was a hole in the wall – *a secret door.* Ella quietly squeaked* in shock and fell backwards. Shaking*, she opened her eyes to find herself in total darkness.

Chapter 5

Rohan searched* outside, hoping to find a river or any other sign of water.

He looked around the gardens but could only see trees, grass, hedges* and lots of weeds*, there was no water anywhere. With a sigh*, he turned back to the house to join Ella.

Suddenly he stopped. In front of the house was a black car.

"Someone else is here," thought Rohan, looking over his shoulder in case* he was being watched.

With his head low*, he hurried back towards the house, past the car and a giant* statue of a teapot and teacup*. He looked through the windows, trying to see if he could spot* Ella or the other visitors.

He jumped at the sound of a woman coming around the house, talking into her mobile phone. The front door was too far away to hurry inside, so he climbed into the stone teacup and hid, breathing* fast.

"It's the woman from the care home," thought Rohan, as he remembered the voice of the angry lady who they had walked into.

Rohan looked down at his shoes and noticed* that he was standing on a pipe* at the bottom of the stone teacup.

He started to feel excited as he realised* that the teapot and teacup were not just statues, but together they were a fountain*. At one point, water would have come out of the teapot into the teacup, where it then went underground* through the pipe.

"Maybe this is one of the water clues* to find a key!" thought Rohan. He looked up to see the woman walking round the other side of the building.

Jumping back out of the teapot, he quickly searched around the fountain, but there was no sign of a key, or any hidden secrets.

Taking a few steps back, he looked up at the teapot from a distance. At the top was a lid with a handle*.

"Maybe there's something inside," thought Rohan. He climbed up onto the side of the teacup and then onto the teapot.

"Hey!" shouted a voice in the distance. Rohan looked up to see the woman hurrying back towards him in black boots. "This is private land! Get down from there!"

Rohan suddenly felt very silly for standing on top of a tall fountain, in full view of anyone who happened to look. He grabbed the lid of the giant teapot, but it was heavy* and difficult to move. His heart beat* fast as he pulled the lid in panic, hoping to get* away from the woman who was just a few feet away.

Chapter 6

“I’ve got you!” shouted the man.

Alicia tried to break* free, but the man was too strong.

“What are you doing here?” he shouted. “I should call the police!”

“What are *you* doing here?” said Alicia, trying to hide the fear* in her voice. She tried to run but the man would not let* go.

At that moment Sammy bit the man’s trouser leg with his teeth and pulled backwards. His arms flapped* in the air as he lost his balance* and fell straight into the pond.

“Gaaaaah!” he screamed, his face covered* in mud, as he tried to get up. He slipped* and fell backwards again.

Alicia ran away with her small dog. “Thanks Sammy!”

They ran back towards the house. Suddenly, Alicia stopped. There was something behind a

group of trees to her left. She turned and came closer*. Behind the trees she saw a small empty swimming pool, with weeds* growing all over the old tiles*.

“The letter was old, and this looks old too,” thought Alicia as her excitement* grew. “Maybe a key is here!” She carefully climbed inside and pulled weeds away from the walls of the empty pool.

At one end of the pool, there was a picture of a teapot. At the other end, there were different shapes* that looked mixed-up*.

Alicia moved around the swimming pool, touching* the tiles. At the deeper end, when she pushed one of the tiles, it moved. She pushed harder and some tiles fell onto the floor. Sammy barked in surprise. *"Woof!"*

As Alicia picked up a tile, she wondered* where to put it. She turned around and looked at the picture of the teapot at the other end and looked at the tiles on the floor.

"These tiles are the same picture, but they were mixed up," she thought. "It's a puzzle!"

Carefully she placed the fallen tiles back on the wall in the shape of a teapot. When she put the last tile back on the wall, another tile opened in the middle of the swimming pool floor. Alicia put her hand inside the hole and pulled out an old metal key.

Chapter 7

Ella's shaking hands felt the walls in the darkness as she found a switch*. She pressed* it and the secret room was filled* with light.

She looked around in surprise. In front of her was another kitchen. The room behind her had been almost empty, but this one was full of old furniture*. There was a wooden table and chairs in the centre. Around the edges* was an old cooker*, sink and cupboards. Shelves on the walls held dusty plates and bowls.

"This is so strange," she thought, "why hide a secret kitchen next to another kitchen?"

Ella walked over to the shelves and picked up a key lying next to a plate.

"That was easy," she thought. She was about to put it in her pocket when she noticed another key further along the shelf. There were even more keys hanging* on the wall.

"How do I know which is the right one?" Ella wondered*. She turned around and explored* the rest of the kitchen. There were keys everywhere – in the sink, in every drawer*, even the cooker had around twenty keys inside.

Ella wondered if she should try to collect all of the keys and put them in her bag. Everywhere she looked there were more keys, even under her feet as she stepped on a few on the dusty floor.

Ella took the letter out and read the lines of the riddle again.

One and two will outside be,
Three is used for stirring tea,*

"*Stirring tea* ...," thought Ella, "... a spoon* ... I have to look for a spoon!" she thought. She ran back to the drawers and pulled out all of the spoons. There were teaspoons, wooden spoons, big spoons and small spoons, but not one of them looked anything like a key.

"Think... think!" said Ella to herself. "I'm missing* something!"

She looked at the riddle again. "Water!"

She turned back to the sink where there was an old unusual-looking tap*, with a long handle* at the back. Grabbing hold of it, she moved the handle up and down. Ella heard a sound from underground* where the water was coming from.

After a few moments water poured from the tap into the sink, bringing with it a long metal object. One end of the object looked like a spoon, while the other end was a key.

"Yes!" cried Ella, grabbing the key before turning to find the others.

Chapter 8

"Get down here – *now!*" screamed the woman from below.

His hands shaking*, Rohan tried one more time to move the teapot lid. Taking a deep breath, he moved it to the side just enough to drop himself into a dark space* below.

Trying not to listen to the woman's shouting, he shone* the light from his phone in the space around him. A large pipe ran through the teapot from the bottom to the top. Opposite the pipe were three clocks on the wall, all set* to twelve o'clock. Above the clocks there were three names, *English Breakfast*, *Darjeeling* and *Oolong*.

Rohan knew that Darjeeling tea came from India, as it was his auntie's favourite tea and she had told him about the city of Darjeeling in India that the tea was named after. Darjeeling was also the city where Rohan's grandparents had lived before they moved to the UK. He also knew that English Breakfast was the name of the tea that his mother drank at home. He quickly looked for 'Oolong' on the internet with his phone. The results told him that Oolong tea came from China. Rohan looked up at the three clocks and touched* them. The hands* on the 'English Breakfast clock' could not be moved past twelve o'clock, but the times on the other two clocks could be changed.

Rohan rubbed* his ear. "Three teas... *hmmm...* three clocks..."

While he was thinking, an angry woman's voice was still shouting at him from outside.

"If 'English Breakfast' is twelve o'clock in the UK, maybe Darjeeling and Oolong are meant to be the times in India and China," thought Rohan. He used his phone to search for the time difference between the countries.

The woman outside became more and more angry. "Get out of there," she shouted. "This is private land!" She stepped into the teacup, trying to climb to the top.

Rohan moved the 'Darjeeling' clock to half past five and the 'Oolong' clock to eight o'clock. As the last clock was moved into place, a loud, rumbling* sound made him jump and the teapot began to shake*.

Outside, the woman heard the rumbling sound, too, which was quickly followed by water pouring out of the teapot straight on top of her.

"Gaaaah!" she screamed, becoming wet* through. Black eye make-up ran down her face as the water rained on her head. "Gaaaah! How... *you... you...* you'll pay for this!" she cried.

She pulled herself out of the teacup and landed on the ground*. Her trouser suit dripped* water as she got to her feet. Reaching* for her bag, she pulled out her phone.

"Jake!" she screamed into her phone as she marched back towards the house. "Jake, get here

now! We need to do something about those kids!"

Rohan used the water pipe to step on and climbed back out of the teapot. He watched as the woman entered the house and pushed the door closed behind her.

Then, he heard the water pouring out of the fountain. He turned to look at it. Hanging* out of the teapot, under the water pipe, was a short bit of rope* holding a key.

Chapter 9

Alicia and Sammy ran to the front of the house where Rohan was holding a key by a fountain*.

"There's a man here," said Alicia, looking at the black car in front of the house. "That must be his car! He caught me, then he *fell* into the pond*!"

"Are you OK?" Rohan asked Alicia, looking a bit worried.

"Sure, sure," Alicia replied. "Sammy saved me," she added, smiling to herself.

At that moment the front door opened and Ella joined the others. "Have you seen other people here?" she asked in a whisper. Then she noticed* the black car.

"It's the man and woman from the care home who saw our letter!" said Rohan. "At least it's the same woman. She went inside, before I found this key."

"I found one too!" said Alicia.

"And me!" Ella reported* happily. "Now what?" she asked. "We have to be very careful with these

two people around," she added. Then Ella took the letter from her bag and read the last two lines:

Take the keys and go today,
To find the treasure, you must lose your way.

Rohan frowned. "How can we find the treasure by losing ourselves?"

"I don't know," said Alicia, "but we might* have to lose* *him*!" A wet* and angry-looking man came towards them.

"I'm going to call Mr Potts," said Ella. "He said we could come here!"

Ella ran in the opposite direction with her mobile phone.

As the man got closer* to the fountain, the front door opened and a woman tipped water out of her left boot onto the front step.

"Jane!" cried the man in surprise. "Did you fall into the pond as well?"

"Of course not, Jake, as if I'd be so stupid! That awful boy turned* the fountain on."

Jake looked up at the fountain, where water was pouring out of a giant* stone teapot into a giant teacup*. "How did the fountain get you wet?"

"I was inside the teacup and..." Jane's face was pink. "Oh, we don't have time for this!" She turned to Rohan, Alicia and Sammy who were backing* away. "Give me that letter!"

"What letter?" asked Alicia, crossing her arms.

"The one the other girl had at the care home, Jake saw it!"

"They've got the keys too," said Jake, "I saw them holding them."

"Hand* them over!" said Jane. "The letter and the keys are mine!"

"And mine!" said Jake, frowning at Jane.

"Shut* up, Jake!" Jane held out her hand to Rohan and Alicia. "Give them to me, now! This is your last chance." Jane and Jake walked forwards.

Chapter 10

"Give me the keys!"

"Never!" cried Alicia.

Sammy did not like anyone shouting at his best friend. He ran forward and barked at the man and woman. *"Woof, woof!"*

Jake stepped away with his hands up. "Be careful Jane," Jake warned, "that dog is a monster! It bit my trousers!"

Jane, still holding her left boot, threw it straight at the dog. She missed*! Sammy picked up the boot and ran back to Alicia with it in his mouth.

"Give that back!" screamed Jane.

Jake and Jane tried to catch Sammy, who was having a lot of fun running between their legs and around them.

At that moment, Ella joined the others again. "Nobody answered*," she whispered, "so I left a message asking them to tell Mr Potts that a man and a woman are here and that we found the keys... What's going on here?" She looked at Jane and Jake who were still trying to catch Sammy.

"We can't get* away yet," said Rohan, "they'd just follow us in the car! We need to split up and lose them, then we can leave with the keys through the front gates."

Alicia called for her dog. "Sammy! Run!"

Chapter 11

Sammy dropped the boot and ran with Alicia away from the fountain, followed by Jake. They ran back past the empty swimming pool and towards the pond.

The man was a fast runner and was soon catching* up with them.

At the pond, Alicia looked over her shoulder. Jake was a few steps behind. In front of them was a wall.

Alicia stopped and put her hands up. Jake stopped in front of the pond, completely out of breath.

“Give... me... the... key...” he gasped*. “You’ve got nowhere*... to... go!”

“Okay, okay.” Alicia slowly took the key out of her pocket and stepped towards Jake. He held out his hand.

At that moment Alicia threw the key up as high as she could. Jake jumped to try to catch it, but it landed close to Sammy who picked it up in his mouth.

Jake ran after Sammy around the pond. As soon as he got close, he threw himself at the dog.

Sammy kicked and wriggled* as Jake tried to pull the key from his mouth. The pair rolled downhill and landed in the pond with a splash.

“Sammy!” cried Alicia in panic as both Sammy and Jake went under the water.

After a few moments, both heads came up.

“Sammy!” Alicia screamed and the little dog swam towards Alicia, the key still in his mouth.

“Oh Sammy!” Alicia picked up her dog and hugged him, before they both ran back towards the front gates.

Chapter 12

Ella ran around the side of the house, past some outdoor buildings. There were old, broken plant pots* and buckets on the ground*.

A tall wall ran around the outside of the garden. Ella noticed a gate in front of her.

As she looked over her shoulder, she saw Jane behind her, but the woman had stopped to put her boot back on.

When Ella ran through the gate, a terrible* smell hit her nose. In front of her were fields, covered in fresh manure*. Holding her nose, she turned around and saw a ladder* against the wall. An idea formed in her head as she remembered a trick that Alicia had played on her. Alicia had put a bucket full of water on the school gate and it had spilled* all over her as she walked through the gate.

Ella ran back into the garden and picked up one of the old buckets. She looked up to see Jane still trying to put her wet boot on.

Going back through the gate, she used the bucket to pick up as much manure as she could. The smell was awful. She climbed up the ladder and carefully put the bucket on the open gate.

Looking over the wall she saw that Jane was standing up.

"I'm over here," said Ella, waving* her arms.

Jane frowned at the girl. "Give me my key!"

"Come and get it!" cried Ella.

Jane ran towards her as Ella quickly climbed back down the ladder and moved a few steps away. When she turned, Jane pushed the gate open and the bucket of stinky manure landed on top of her head.

"Gaaaah!" screamed Jane, whose hair, head and shoulders were covered* in brown manure. "You won't get* away with this! Wait till I get you!"

Ella held onto her sides with laughter, before running around back to the front gates of Tea Towers.

Chapter 13

Rohan ran to one side of the house. After a few moments he turned and saw that Jane and Jake were not chasing* him.

He turned and walked back to the front door, deciding to look for his friends to see what was going on.

A few minutes later he heard voices coming from behind the house.

“When I find those children, I'll make them pay!” shouted Jane. “And that dog!” she added. “The keys and the treasure are mine!”

“Hey! They are mine...,” Jake begun, “— there he is!” Jake suddenly noticed Rohan who ran inside the house.

“Give me the key!” screamed Jane.

Rohan reached* the top of the stairs just as the front door was opening and hid behind a wall.

"I wish I hadn't come into the house," he thought. "It's going to be hard to escape* two of them!"

He heard footsteps downstairs as Jane and Jake went to search* the ground floor* of the building. He moved quietly, looking in each of the bedrooms. There was nowhere* to hide, as there was no furniture* in any of the rooms.

At the end of the corridor he opened a door. There was another staircase. He quietly closed the door behind him and went upstairs.

At the top of the long narrow* staircase there was another door. Rohan turned the key in the lock* and opened it. Fresh air hit his face and dark hair as he stepped outside onto the roof.

Rohan could see the whole of Tea Towers' garden. He could not see Alicia, Sammy and Ella, but he noticed something else: On one side of the garden was a maze* made out of green hedges*.

Suddenly Rohan remembered the last line of the riddle.

To find the treasure, you must lose your way.

“People get lost in a maze... of course,” thought Rohan. “That’s where we need to go!”

But first Rohan needed to get out of the house without Jane and Jake catching him. He looked over the edge* of the roof, wondering* if he could climb down. It looked very dangerous.

He was about to leave through the door when it suddenly opened. He heard Jane and Jake talking to each other. Quickly, he hid behind a chimney*.

Jane and Jake had found him...

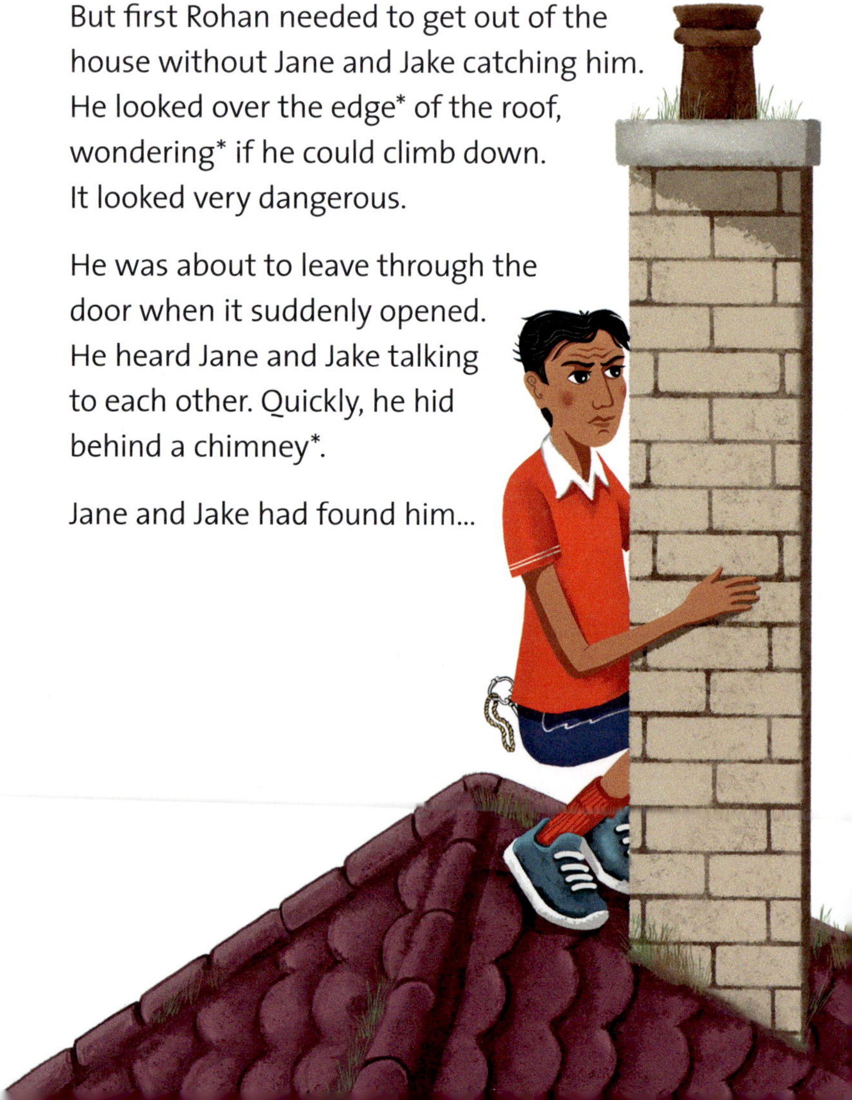

"He's not here," said Jake.

"I can see that!" said Jane, her voice angry. "He must have got out. Let's see if we can see him down there."

Rohan heard the pair walk over to the side of the roof. Glancing* at the open door, he took his chance and ran back through it.

"Hey!" yelled Jane's voice behind him.

With shaking hands, Rohan closed the door and tried to turn* the key. It fell out of the lock onto the floor.

Breathing fast, Rohan picked up the key as footsteps pounded* towards the door. He pushed the key back in the lock and turned it again. This time, it worked. Sighing, Rohan ran downstairs to find the others.

Chapter 14

Rohan ran out the front door as Alicia, Sammy and Ella were calling his name outside the house.

“There you are!” said Ella. “We were waiting at the front gate! Alicia pushed Jake in the pond and Jane got covered in manure*, but we don’t know where they are now.”

“We should get out of here,” said Alicia.

Rohan smiled. “It’s okay, they’re locked* on the roof! They both came looking for me.”

“Wow!” Ella was surprised. “Now we need to work out the last bit of the riddle... *‘to find the treasure, you must lose your way’*.”

“I think I worked that out too!” Rohan looked to his left. “There’s a maze* over there, I saw it from the roof.”

“That’s it!” cried Alicia.

At that moment another car pulled up on the drive.

“Oh no ... Not more visitors!” cried Rohan.

A man and woman got out of the car and went to the back of the car to help a man in a wheelchair.

“It’s Mr Potts!” said Alicia.

The two carers pushed his wheelchair around to the group.

"We got your message," said one of the carers to Ella, "and Mr Potts was very worried and said we had to come here."

"Yes I did," said Mr Potts, frowning. "Where are my niece* and nephew?"

All three opened their mouths in shock.

"Jane and Jake are your... family?" said Rohan.

Mr Potts sighed. "Sadly, yes, they are! For two years they've been trying to make me hand* over Tea Towers to them, saying that they would pay for my care home fees* if I did. But I didn't believe them and so they tried to say the building wasn't safe*! But I will never give Tea Towers to them, they would just pull* it down and build flats. This place means a lot to me, it's been in my family for a long time. I can still see it from my window up on the hill and I don't want it pulled down."

"That's terrible*," said Ella, feeling sorry for Mr Potts who she thought must have felt quite lonely with his family trying to trick* him.

"Today, at the care home," explained Mr Potts, "they suddenly started asking me questions about a treasure. I didn't tell them anything but it made me worried. Another reason why I wanted to come here ... but you didn't answer my question..." Mr Potts looked around. "Where are they?"

"Uncle Arthur!" a voice made them all jump as Jane looked down from the roof. "Let us out!"

Mr Potts was surprised. "We'll let you out," said Mr Potts, "only if you never visit me or Tea Towers ever again!"

"Mr Potts!" Alicia touched* the old man's shoulder. "You have to come with us! We know where the treasure is!"

Chapter 15

The two carers went to free Jane and Jake from the roof, while Alicia, Rohan and Ella pushed Mr Potts' wheelchair into the middle of the maze.

"There's nothing here," said Mr Potts.

"But there has to be something," said Rohan.

"Wait..." said Ella. "The riddle said we have to *lose ourselves*... so we shouldn't be in the middle of the maze, we need to look at the dead* ends!"

They all split up to search* the dead ends of the maze for any sign of a secret door.

"Have you found anything yet?" called Rohan to the others.

"No!" shouted Alicia.

Ella was exploring* a corner of the maze with Mr Potts when the wheel* of his chair hit something.

“Something’s down there,” said Mr Potts.

Ella pulled the wheelchair backwards. On the ground she could see metal through the dirt*.

“Alicia! Rohan! Come over here!”

She pushed the dirt away to find a metal door with three keyholes*. Alicia, Rohan and Ella each put a key inside the locks and turned. The door sprang* open, with a ramp* below.

"This is so exciting!" said Rohan, as they carefully pushed Mr Potts' wheelchair down the ramp. In front of them was a large metal door with words in black:

Under the words was a combination* lock with spaces for six letters.

"We need a tea with six letters," said Ella, looking at Mr Potts.

"Wilfred Potts was my grandfather," he said, "I was just a boy when he died. He loved tea... but I can't remember his favourite tea."

"Let's try oolong," said Rohan. He moved the letters to spell the word. The door did not move.

"Jasmine?" said Alicia.

"That's seven letters," said Ella.

Mr Potts scratched* his head. "He always drank tea with ginger* biscuits... that's it! Ginger!"

Rohan moved the letters again to spell 'ginger'. The metal door flew open with a loud *bang*. Behind the door was a dark room.

Sammy ran inside, followed by everyone else. Rohan and Ella shone* lights from their phones around the room. Shelves* from top to bottom were filled with golden teapots, teacups and statues.

"Wow!" cried Alicia. "Look at all this treasure!" She went to a small golden box in the corner of the room. "There's something written on this box ... *Da-Hong Pao...*"

Mr Potts gasped*. "Da-Hong Pao is the most expensive tea in the world! It's worth* millions!"

"Don't touch it, Alicia!" cried Ella, afraid* that her sister would drop the expensive tea.

TEA

Tea
1882
Don't touch it Alicia!

"There's something else here..." said Rohan, opening a wooden box that was full of photos. He handed some to Mr Potts.

"These are all my family's treasures and memories," said Mr Potts, a tear* falling from his eye. "You children have no idea how much this means to me."

After exploring the treasure, they decided to lock it back in the room until everything could be moved to a safe place.

"What are you going to do with Tea Towers now?" Ella asked Mr Potts, when they were back at the car. "You've got enough money now to live here with people to look after you!"

Mr Potts shook* his head. "I'm an old man now, this place is too much for me and I have no other family. I'll make sure it goes to someone who can restore* it to the beautiful house it once was. But these memories and these photos will stay with me forever... and I'm so thankful that you children found them."

When they returned to the two carers, Jane and Jake's car was gone. Ella, Rohan and Alicia said goodbye and promised to visit Mr Potts again.

"It's funny isn't it," said Ella, as they went to get their bikes. "All that gold and expensive tea... and all Mr Potts really cared* about was getting his family photos back."

"That's his real treasure I guess," said Rohan.

"This is my real treasure," said Alicia, showing her phone which she had used to take pictures of the treasure room. "Wait till we tell Mum and Dad about this!"

"You know what," Rohan suddenly wondered, "we never did find out who this *Ted Wiltforps* guy* was who wrote the riddles..."

Both Alicia and Ella shrugged*. “Race you there!” said Ella.

They rode their bikes back down the hill to the village with Sammy running alongside them, leaving the treasure of Tea Towers behind them.

1. Auflage 1 [5 4 3 2 1] | 2025 24 23 22 21

www.klett-sprachen.de

Autor: Jemma Hatt
Redaktion: Don Haupt
Layoutkonzeption: Maja Merz
Illustrationen: Andrew Smith
Gestaltung und Satz: Joachim Schrimm, ETYPO, Friolzheim
Umschlaggestaltung: Eva Lettenmayer
Titelbild: Andrew Smith
Druck und Bindung: Plump Druck & Medien GmbH,
Rheinbreitbach

Printed in Germany
ISBN 978-3-12-530909-8

9 783125 309098